35 Tips for Students to Succeed in Corporate America

Sharon A. Hill

ISBN: 978-1-4303-2955-8

Online editions may also be available for this title. For more information visit www.lulu.com.

Acknowledgements

I have an amazing network of friends and business associates — so many of them contributed to the creation of this book.

My thanks to Martin and Barbara Brossman, Lorana Price of Holy Cow Branding, Julio Vazquez, Kathleen O'Toole of KO Graphic Design, Debbie Morrison, Dr. Bala Ram, Cari (CareBear) Willis, Stephanie Hlavin, and, of course, my amazing husband, Elmer T. Hill.

Table of Contents

Forward

Sharon Hill is a powerhouse committed to walking her talk and asking the hard questions about what really works in the world. She listens; she observes; she has lived it. She has made her share of mistakes, and she is on a clear path to give back to society through her smart, insightful material that you can use right this minute. If you have not seen or heard her speak, I hope you will someday. At minimum you will hear her voice in the words of this book.

Having grown up inside the District of Columbia in Washington, I was the Caucasian minority-of-one in my classes for many years, which blessed me with a unique perspective. After high school, I chose to go St. Andrews College in a small town in North Carolina – a totally different perspective than that offered by my childhood. I then later went to work for IBM. This range of experiences made me appreciate the subtle and not-so-subtle differences of these diverse environments.

Now, as a Success Coach and trainer of coaches in Raleigh, NC, I meet daily with men and women who could benefit from Sharon's solid advice in the pages of this book. Too bad that Sharon had not yet compiled this wisdom when I was passing through the stages from high school to college to the corporate world—it would have been immensely helpful! This book is a powerful tool for successfully transiting the academic years and transitioning to business.

I urge you to absorb Sharon's practical advice. You'll find this book to be more than just another set of useful ideas you let pass through your head. This dedicated woman is giving sound advice from personal history and research that will enhance your life. Take it on, especially the stuff you may not agree with, and try it out. Test it through your own experience in the real world and see what you learn. It is often when we step outside our comfort zone that we truly grow and learn the most. I personally find the times when I have been proven wrong have been doorways to the greatest growth in life. This book is packed with the kind of wisdom you may not get from family and friends, especially if they have not been down the road you're traveling. It will give you the greatest value – if only you use it.

I think there's no limit to who can benefit from this book, including people who are currently in corporate jobs and not satisfied with their progress. So readers, take special note where Sharon discusses the value of finding a good mentor. I hope you recognize she is providing some excellent mentoring right here in these dynamic pages – this book is a joy to read!

Martin Brossman, Success Coach
(www.coachingsupport.com)

Introduction

The original goal of this Common Sense Handbook was to provide tips for succeeding in corporate America. I obtained my corporate experience at IBM where I worked in Marketing, Product Development, and stints as an Executive Assistant. While in management, I saw so many employees torpedo their careers because of misguided assumptions about how to succeed in corporate America that I was intrigued and curious as to why this was happening, so I researched the question for my M.B.A. thesis.

Most of the information in this book is based on my research and comments from my research volunteers and friends.

You will find this book easy to read. I have written this book using straightforward talk. My goal is to write so that you can understand and learn. You have no time to read? How about reading one tip a day?

Although this book is targeted to students as you prepare for corporate America, I know some of you plan to take a different path. You may want to start your own business, work for a non-profit business or organization, go into the military, or become a writer. Regardless, this book gives you information to share with others to help them in their corporate quest.

Section 1. Welcome to your New Job.

As a student, your goal is probably to get through college with a decent GPA and start working in corporate America. You want to make a decent wage and be promoted to positions of power. How hard can it be?

I have news. It is very difficult to attain those goals unless you already know how to practice the tips I present in this book. Let's get started.

.

Tip 1

Focus on What You Know. Learn the Processes.

Focus on What You Know. Learn the Processes.

When you start a new job, your first priority is to learn and do the job you were hired to do. Learn the processes and apply your knowledge. If you are not assigned a mentor, observe how employees interact with each other, how they react to you, what spoken and unspoken rules prevail and how close people are to each other. If your current job processes are different than those you learned in college, you have no choice but to be flexible and master the new processes.

MBA's have a special challenge in this area. Many corporations hire MBA's expecting them to arrive running. Corporations assume the new MBA employee needs little guidance because of their educational background. I've personally seen a group of MBA's arrive to find a telephone, desktop computer, and organization chart in their cubicles. They had no mentors or documented processes. How could they possibly be productive? Some quit in frustration. Others were proactive about taking control of an impossible situation. They used their assertion skills to network and find the right people to talk to. Their goal was simple. They needed to discover what their job was and how they were going to be measured.

Here is a tip. If you get no responses to questions about your job responsibilities and how you will be measured, evaluate if you want to stay in that job. Avoid getting an ulcer the size of Texas because you are caught in a catch-22. The higher the salary you're given, the less support management will think you need.

Tip 2

As You Rise, Focus on Whom You Know.

As You Rise, Focus on Whom You Know.

A promotion means more responsibility and longer hours. It also means your results are scrutinized much more. You advanced because of what you know and how you sold yourself. Good job. Now, it gets tougher.

Now is the time to ensure you have a vast network of contacts, experts, and those who know the politics of an organization. Have a few people you can turn to and depend on for straight answers and advice.

Do you know the difference between a mentor and a sponsor? You find your mentors. Your sponsors find you. A sponsor is someone who realizes your potential and wants to groom you for higher levels of success. Like it or not, in the workplace, you are always being watched. Therefore, it's critical not to burn bridges, always be professional, and turn in positive, if not measurable, results.

By focusing on whom you know, you have inside information from those in the know who are aware of your areas of interest (and corresponding opportunities), pitfalls to avoid, and how to play the corporate game smarter.

Don't disappoint them by not following their advice. If a person feels you are wasting his or her time, they will drop you. I mentored a gentleman who wanted to talk once a month for one hour. After four months I noticed he had not implemented one of the ideas we agreed he try. I dropped him. It may sound cold, but I didn't want to be involved with someone who did not appreciate my time or advice. This gave me insights into his character and I decided I didn't want my name associated with him.

Instead, I opened up the mentoring slot to another person who was eager to gobble up and apply my ideas.

George Fraser, world-famous speaker; author; and founder of the annual PowerNetworking Conference, says that it is not enough to focus on whom you know. Mr. Fraser emphasizes that you must also focus on who knows <u>you</u> and what they know about you. He urges his audiences to "be careful who your friends are. Don't spend major time with minor people."

Minor people are not minor because of their professions. They are minor because of bad behavior, misguided attitudes toward life, and continued bad judgment. If you are associated with minor people, it could come back to haunt you. The words you speak and the deeds you do today are waiting for you tomorrow.

Tip 3

Learn the Politics
and the Players.

Learn the Politics and the Players.

This may be the most uncomfortable task you have to do, especially if you are an introvert. But it is a must-do for employees who want an edge in retaining their jobs. There are no guarantees for holding on to your job, especially when companies start downsizing. Hopefully, if your company does downsize, you'll be one of the last to leave or escape the layoffs because you were savvy about the politics and protected yourself.

Start by finding out who has the power in the organization. It's not always the manager. Then, find out what that person believes are the rules for acceptable behavior in the organization. This is powerful because there is no set formula for how to go about this, yet it's critical to keeping your job.

The sooner you realize and practice acceptable behavior, the sooner you can bridge the gap.

If the rules for acceptable behavior are in line with your principles, practice them. For example, if lunch is 45 minutes, don't take an hour every day. If working at home is allowed as long as employees check in with their manager on a daily basis, so be it.

However, if the rules offend you, it's time to make a career decision. If sexist behavior is allowed in a good-old-boy system, ask yourself if you are willing to sell out.

Tip 4

Involve Yourself with Your Team.

Involve Yourself with Your Team.

Managers look for team players in an organization. Being a team player is as important as demonstrating leadership skills. This could put you outside your comfort zone if you did not learn team skills in college.

Believe it or not, you can make more friends in a shorter time by becoming interested in other people rather than trying to get other people interested in you.

Here are some simple tips that I find effective:

Smile… smile and continue to smile. It costs nothing, enriches those who receive it, and happens in a flash but the memory lasts forever. A smile cannot be bought, begged, or borrowed; it comes from the heart. If you want other people to like you, make the other person feel important – and do it sincerely!

Some people thrive on arguments even though it gives them a sour disposition and creates a depressing atmosphere around them. The only way to get the best of an argument is to avoid it. If you are wrong, admit it quickly and apologize. If the other person continues in an argumentative manner, excuse yourself and walk away. As the saying goes, don't bite.

There are four categories of conversation in which you never want to participate: politics, religion, how to spend your money, and how to raise your kids. Trust me, with these subjects, tempers flare easily, and just about no one feels good at the end.

Be sincerely interested in what others have to say. Look them in the eye. Listen carefully. Ask questions. Empathize. Laugh (with them, not at them). In short, be good company.

Finally, be yourself. This is a growth experience and takes time to nurture.

Tip 5

Continue Learning.

Continue Learning.

You have your graduate or undergraduate degree and now that you have your new job, are celebrating that you are finished with hitting the books. But wait. Nothing could be further from the truth. In corporate America, you are expected to stay on top of technology, trends, the marketplace — topics that are relevant and unique to your industry, and all other areas that affect your productivity and personal growth.

Whether or not your company pays for classes or advanced study, you must continue learning to stay vital and current.

My friend, Debbie M., told me about a student who started his college career as an English major and before graduation, changed to Marketing. Following school, he wants to join a corporation and has assumed that what he learned in college is all he needs.

As a person who has worked for years in corporate America, Debbie was talking to him about technology behemoths Cisco and IBM and what marketing people do in those organizations. The student had no idea about how marketing varies depending upon what you are selling and to whom. Also, he knew nothing about a computer except how to use a word processor. It never occurred to him that he might need to know something about how to strategically use the Internet for market intelligence or that the web itself could be a marketing tool.

The student may be graduating but, clearly, he has a lot more learning to do.

Tip 6

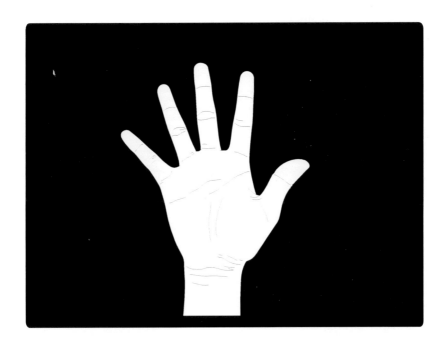

**Volunteer for
Assignments That
People Want to Avoid.**

Volunteer for Assignments That People Want to Avoid.

Have you ever heard the term brown-noser? The Dictionary of American Slang labels brown-noser as taboo and defines it as, "to curry favor with a superior." The image that generated this expression is of an underling who kisses a superior, but not on the mouth, and gets his or her nose dirty as a consequence.

This tip involves working beyond your job to make yourself and your manager look good. Many of those who are less ambitious and jealous may accuse you of brown-nosing. What an obnoxious taunt! I say ignore them. You can wave down at them when you reach the corporate mountaintop.

Following are two scenarios to consider.

Scenario #1: Your manager needs someone to learn ISO 9000 and train the department. This task will take at least six months and is **in addition** to the volunteer's regular job responsibilities. The typical first reaction to a request like this is to take a giant step backwards and say, "No, thank you." Everyone is already busy. Why complicate the job by adding more hours and more work? And what the heck is ISO 9000?

But think for a minute. This is your manager asking. The task may be difficult and stressful, but if you can do it and do it WELL, what a feather in your cap it will be. Volunteer. Here is how you get started:

1. Set time with your manager to understand:
   - ❑ Objective
   - ❑ Timeframe
   - ❑ Contacts
   - ❑ Known obstacles

2. Discuss your current workload. Can you get relief in some areas? If not, tell your manager how many hours you will be able to devote to the task, keeping in mind you must make the target end date.
3. Create your project plan. Include weekly updates with management. Updates include not only status, but also areas in which you need help.
4. Put your time management skills in place. Your regular job must not suffer.
5. Do not be afraid to say you don't understand if you run into a roadblock. Remember, "Pride goeth before the fall." If you don't speak up when you have problems, you are doomed to fail.
6. Get buy-in from your team. Can someone assist with training? Give credit to those who help you.
7. Do not be intimidated by those at a higher level. If they have the information you need to complete the task, talk to them.
8. Be sure to eat properly and try to get enough sleep. If you don't, you will compound your stress.
9. Document your process and hold on to those notes. When the task is completed, refer to your notes when it is time for your performance review.

Congratulations! If you survived, you proved you are not a brown-noser. You are a professional who is following the tips for success.

Scenario #2: Your manager needs someone to handle the charitable contribution program for your department. The task involves getting all your team members to return the contribution cards, even if they are not donating.

This task is 90% easier than the first scenario, but the results are similar. Volunteer. You are unloading a task from your manager. This puts you in a positive spotlight. The point is the same: large or small, time-consuming or not, volunteering for jobs no one else wants gets you in front of leadership and positions you alongside the higher level team members.

Although this task is not critical for the department's success, your volunteering shows your leadership skills and teamwork. Be sure to mention the volunteer assignment when it comes time for your performance review.

Tip 7

Eat Lunch with Others, Especially if They Don't Look Like You.

Eat Lunch with Others, Especially if They Don't Look Like You.

Birds of a feather flock together means that people who are similar to each other often spend time together.

It's true, it is easier to be around people who look like you and have similar interests. You're in your comfort zone. Although being in your comfort zone is easy and fun, did you know that if you **only** hang with those like you, you are limiting your cultural growth and, perhaps, your career? I have seen people taken out of management because:

- They didn't know how to relate to the different ethnicities within their department
- They said sexist things to women and vice versa, to men
- They gave all the plum assignments to those that looked like them, ignoring more qualified people because they were uncomfortable around them
- They used inappropriate terminology with other races

By going to lunch with others that don't look like you, you gain a wealth of ethnic information, learn to appreciate your differences, and gain a comfort level that will help you in your career.

Get the book *Ouch! That Stereotype Hurts* by Leslie C. Aguilar to learn how to communicate respectfully in a diverse world. I consider it a must-read.

Tip 8

Make Yourself
Valuable.

Make Yourself Valuable.

Your boss will do whatever it takes to keep you on board if you make him or her look good by producing strong results. By finishing grunt work, identifying and solving problems, and improving or creating services and products, you will have an advantage over the competition, says Bruce Tulgan, founder of Rainmaker Thinking, a Connecticut consultancy group.

"Every single skill you get under your belt, every single relationship you build with a decision maker who knows you're valuable, every single ounce of strength you add to your brain, body and spirit become cards in your hand," says Tulgan. "Those are chips in your pile that you can use to trade for rewards in your career."

How can you make yourself valuable in tangible ways? Learn a relevant foreign language, pick up technical skills or produce top-notch research. Possessing soft skills — ranging from the capacity to learn quickly to the ability to communicate well — doesn't hurt either. Instead of networking in the traditional sense, use the skills you have to make yourself valuable to someone with whom you'd like to build a relationship; then, perhaps he or she will be more willing to help you in the future, says Tulgan.

Keep yourself marketable not just in your company but externally as well. What if your company has a massive layoff? If you have built relationships with people of value in other companies outside your company, you have a network that, if they know your value, opens doors for job opportunities.

Want to hear the fast path to failure? Just say, "That's not part of my job description." Everyone needs to set limits, but doing only the bare minimum sends a clear message that you're just interested in a regular paycheck. Sooner or later, your boss will start looking for someone willing to take more initiative.

Tip 9

Attract Attention.

Attract Attention.

Greet problems as friends. Problems you solve get you noticed by the powers that be. If you're not tackling problems, you are missing opportunities for growth. Gain recognition as an expert problem solver and the word will spread fast.

Tip 10

Find Your Passion.

Find Your Passion.

Enjoying your work is a great motivator. You can't sleepwalk through your job. Carol Kuc, president of the National Association of Women Business Owners speaks to all when she says, "If you have passion, you'll give your work full attention, and you'll find success."

Finding your passion can translate into acting entrepreneurially at your existing company. Present new ideas, take ownership of projects and increase your responsibilities. See Tip 6, *Volunteer for Assignments that People Want to Avoid.* Sooner or later, that kind of devotion will lead to a promotion – maybe even two or three.

I always found passion learning to become an expert. I got satisfaction when others came to me to solve problems because they heard that I'm an expert. If I had on-going questions about a certain topic, I held intra-company seminars to share my knowledge. I provided handouts and made sure everyone knew I was available to them for questions.

My passion to become an expert helped the organization become more productive and I got positive attention from top management.

Tip 11

Keep Your
Sense of Humor.

Keep Your Sense of Humor.

Having a sense of humor and refraining from taking yourself too seriously is an important part of succeeding in the workforce. Laughing attracts people and will help get you promoted.

You'll have an easier time getting ahead if you're a pleasure to work with. "If you have a reputation for being difficult, rude, and unethical or unreasonably demanding, you will inevitably be passed on for someone who creates less friction on a team," says Jennifer Kwee, who is the product marketing manager at Motorola in Libertyville, IL.

Being likable requires you to be happy. Feeling satisfied and fulfilled means finding balance between your personal life and work as much as possible. Getting burned out won't help you get promoted. In fact, it just might hurt your chances of moving forward.

Tip 12

Get a Mentor –
Especially One That
Does Not Look
Like You.

Get a Mentor – Especially One That Does Not Look Like You.

Looking for a boost in your job search or working life? A mentor is the one person who can guide you, help you, take you under his or her wing, and nurture your career quest. What separates a mentor from the average network contact is long-term commitment and a deep-seated investment in your future. When you have a mentor, you are the protégé.

Where a typical networking contact might be associated with quick introductions, exchanges of business cards, and phone calls, your relationship with a mentor likely involves long lunches and time spent in the mentor's office. A mentor is often in a position you'd like to be in and has the clout and connections to guide you to a similar position. He or she is someone you probably have unusually good chemistry with; who will share stories with you of his or her own climb to success. An effective mentor isn't afraid to criticize constructively, so be sure you are not thin-skinned when receiving honest and constructive criticism about yourself.

When you have an appointment with your mentor, keep it. I have received complaints from mentors that protégés do not honor the commitment that is made with their mentor. Some protégés do not practice common etiquette of alerting the mentor that they have a scheduling conflict and will have to reschedule. Another complaint is that the mentor and protégé have an agreement about tasks the protégé should do, but the protégé doesn't follow up. For example, the mentor and protégé agree that the protégé will set up a courtesy interview with a manager to understand the skills needed to move into the manager's department. Months pass and the protégé never calls the manager for an appointment. The protégé has just violated the mentor/protégé contract.

Finding a mentor

Check first to see whether your current employer, your college alma mater, or other organization with which you're associated already has a formal mentoring program in place. In these structured arrangements, participants are sometimes given personality assessments so that protégés can be matched with compatible mentors. Other organizations have found that when mentors and protégés are very different, greater opportunities for discovery emerge. That is why it is so important to include mentors who do not look like you. This may mean stepping out of your comfort zone. Why can't a black man have a white woman for a mentor? Why can't an Asian woman have a white man for a mentor? If your mentor is in a position to help you and has a wide network, your goal is to work with that person and learn.

To find a mentor on your own, identify someone you admire and respect. You can choose someone from your own place of employment or outside it — or both — some people have more than one mentor. Serial mentors, those mentors with whom you have a short-term relationship, one after the other, work well for some people. In an article on the CareerJournal.com Website, authors Beverly Kaye and Devon Scheef state that short-term mentoring relationships comprise "mentworking," a process combining mentoring and networking and enabling participants to give and receive in relationships in which everyone is both learner and teacher. "You'll…be sharing your knowledge and abilities with others," the authors write, "serving as a mentor to many. In other words, each 'mentworker' receives and gives brain power to others, creating multiple short-term learning teams."

Decide what you need in a mentor – what skills you'd like to develop with your mentor's assistance. Consider your goals in choosing a mentor. Think about what characteristics you're looking for in a mentor. You may want to do a bit of sleuthing to find out what the prospective mentor is like. What is his or her communication style? Ask the would-be mentor's co-workers and subordinates for their insights.

It's a good idea to choose someone working in the same functional area as you are, as well as someone who shares your values. Professional organizations in your field, whether they offer formal mentoring programs or not, can be excellent sources of mentors. Test the waters by asking advice. Be sure to reveal as much of yourself as possible. Mentors are most likely to invest themselves in those in whom they see a little of themselves, which is why you should never approach a prospective mentor in a state of desperation or helplessness.

Don't ask your direct supervisor to be your mentor; it's better to have someone with whom you can talk freely about career and workplace issues. Some protégés prefer an older, more experienced mentor at a higher organizational level so they, too, can aspire to the upper echelons of the career ladder, while others benefit from peer mentors. *Fast Company* magazine offers the story of Lourdes Townsend who worked with 20 peer mentors as part of a program sponsored by her employer, Stride Rite. "I never thought about learning from someone on my level," Townsend says. "I always looked two to four levels above me and wondered what I had to do to get there. But the people who have the best solutions to the problems I face are often the people facing those problems themselves."

What to look for in a mentor

A mentor wants to work with someone he or she can respect. He or she may even desire to mold the protégé in his or her own image, which is fine as long as the mentor is not too obsessive about it, and you are comfortable with the image into which you're being molded. In that sense, a mentor can be a role model —someone you'd like to model yourself after — but does not have to be.

Women and members of minorities that are underrepresented in the workplace may find it especially helpful to seek out mentors and role models of the same background so they can identify with the success of someone who has made it in a diverse workforce, as well as having a mentor who looks different.

You should have a good feel after a few meetings as to whether the rapport is right for a mentoring relationship. At that point, you can either come right out or ask the person to be your mentor, if that feels appropriate, or you can simply tell him or her how much you've benefited from their wisdom imparted so far and you hope he or she will continue to share it with you.

You should bring trustworthiness and the ability to keep confidences to the mentoring relationship, suggests Women Unlimited. The group also suggests that mentored relationships benefit when the protégé approaches the mentoring with openness, honesty, introspection, realistic expectations, accountability, and the ability to admit mistakes and share failures. Look for similar qualities in a mentor, the group advises, as well as a sense of humor, good listening skills, a high comfort level in giving feedback, and the ability to discuss a wide range of issues. Jeffrey Patnaude, author of *Leading from the Maze*, also suggests that mentors possess emotional intelligence, intuition, a drive to keep learning, and a desire to bring about change. Avoid a mentor who is too controlling, judgmental, or a know-it-all. Look for a positive, upbeat attitude – someone who will become invested in and celebrate your successes. The mentorship is especially productive when the mentor believes he or she can learn from you, and the relationship is a two-way street.

Mentors can be from outside your company as well as inside your company. Open your search for a mentor by finding potential mentors within professional organizations, conferences, and on-line networking programs.

54

Nurturing the mentoring relationship

Talk with your mentor about mutual expectations for the mentoring relationship – how it will work, what it will look like, and how often you'll communicate. You and your mentor may want to agree at the outset that either of you can end the relationship at any time with no hard feelings. Also, be sure not to overburden your mentor by demanding too much time and attention or becoming overly dependent on your mentor. Some experts suggest monthly meetings supplemented by regular e-mail and phone contact. Your meetings can be in the workplace, over a meal, at the gym, or anyplace that's conducive to a productive exchange of ideas. Set boundaries relating to confidentiality, time commitments, and the areas you mutually feel the mentor can most help you with.

The mentor may tend to give a lot more than you do to the relationship, so be sure to express regularly that you value and appreciate your mentor's guidance. The feeling of being needed and making a difference in a protégé's life will often be a rewarding payoff for the mentor, but don't be afraid to supplement that reward with a token gift, flowers, or by picking up the check when you share a meal. You could also send a note to the mentor's supervisor praising his or her contribution to your professional growth.

You'll know if the mentoring relationship is working if your mentor encourages your goals, provides honest and constructive feedback, helps you develop self-awareness, challenges you to grow beyond your perceived limitations, introduces you to movers and shakers, motivates you to join professional organizations that can help you advance, and above all, listens to you and is easy to communicate with.

What's in it for the mentor?

Your mentor is going to take time from an obviously busy schedule to work with you. Think about what you have to offer your mentor. Mentors get satisfaction in seeing you follow up with your agreements. They take pride in knowing that you are growing because of their help and that they are not wasting their time and see value in the relationship they have with you. Also, think of how you can help your mentor. Can you open doors for them in any way? Get to know them and try to determine a way to help them.

What do mentors do?

Your mentor can help you assess your strengths and weaknesses, as well as help you develop skills for success and a long-range career plan. If you and your mentor share the same employer, your mentor can foster your sense of belonging within the organization, help you navigate the company culture and politics, as well as let you know who the organization's key players are. You can also work through career and workplace issues with your mentor's assistance. A mentor can provide a fresh perspective, a new way of looking at a problem or issue. You can bounce ideas off your mentor. Look for a relationship in which the mentor is more coach than adviser – one in which the mentor facilitates your decision-making process by suggesting alternatives rather than telling you what to do. Ideally, your mentor will motivate you to do your best work.

Tip 13

Learn to Sell
Yourself.

Learn to Sell Yourself.

Another secret to a successful career is to sell yourself. Become known as an expert on a subject. Know your subject inside out, upside down, backward and forward. Study it tirelessly, endlessly, relentlessly. Love your passion. And make it a passion that knows no bounds and has no limits. Devote yourself to your field resolutely — and make yourself its master. Dedicate your energy, your time, and your resources without limit and without reserve to your chosen discipline. When you share your expertise with others, be sure to let upper management know that you have been an unselfish team player. Yes, have a love affair with your career and it will produce both satisfaction and wealth.

Also, to sell yourself to others, you should know your values. Know your value and don't settle for less. Know what you stand for. Know what truly matters, bone-deep, to you. Know where you've been. Know where you're going. Know why you do what you do.

It is not your manager's job to keep track of all the good deeds and amazing results you achieve. It is your job to keep your management chain informed of the value you are providing for their investment in you. Corporations are moving away from regular activity reports. Create one for yourself anyway. Keep notes on your accomplishments in a journal. Share these accomplishments with your management team either periodically or during your performance reviews. Make it easy for your manager to know your value.

Tip 14

Dress Professionally.

Dress Professionally.

When you first enter corporate America, you probably have not built your professional wardrobe. The business world has become much more casual. In some companies, the majority of employees work at home and rarely see each other.

Regardless, there will be times when you will meet with upper management or customers and want to make a positive impression.

The following thoughts reveal what others may be thinking about you, especially for first impressions.[1]

Self-esteem

How you dress is your love of self, made tangible to the world. When you wear ill-fitting, soiled, torn, tattered clothing, it can make others aware of a poor sense of self-worth. What people see on the outside lets them know how you feel about yourself on the inside. Image is the tip of the iceberg, yet it adds immeasurably to helping people understand what's going on inside you.

Self-respect

How you wear it and what you choose to wear shows others how much you respect yourself. Few people come even close to naturally having a perfect shape or size. Those who respect themselves know how to dress to emphasize strengths and minimize body flaws. Respect for self is lacking in women in the workplace who wear skirts that are too short, necklines that are too low, pants that are too tight; men who wear pants that are too short, ties with spots, jeans with holes; with anyone who gains weight and

---

[1] *Dress for Success: Creating a Professional Image*, Lillian D. Bjorseth

then wears clothes that used to fit. Self-respect plays a big part in knowing and wearing the acceptable thing socially and professionally.

Confidence

The way you carry yourself contributes greatly to the air of confidence others perceive. What you wear also contributes to that look of confidence. When I wear a hat, inevitably men and women will say to me they love the confidence I portray. Some women say they would love to wear hats but are afraid they can't carry it off. Men and women both say how a hat completes a woman's outfit. Your goal is to create an aura of confidence and assuredness when you walk into a room. Make sure your clothing contributes its part!

Organizational skills

Even people who don't like to file or plan the details of an event need to appear organized in their clothing color and style choices. You want to create a unified look from head to foot, without calling attention to any one item or color.

Soundness of judgment

Knowing and wearing the right outfit for the right occasion is an important indicator of whether you can make the right decisions at work, too. Lillian Bjorseth wrote that when she attended a business leads group and held after-hour events, most of the attendees wore suits or business-casual wear. The member who owned a singles dating service and came attired in black velvet slacks, a rhinestone-studded strapless top, and a black shawl turned more than one eye! She may have been dressed appropriately for one of her events, but not for a business event. She made a statement, but it is doubtful it was the one she wanted to make. Know when to wear a suit, business casual or formal attire to blend in appropriately.

Attention to detail

In business, about 90 percent of your body is clothed. The remaining 10 percent of your impression is made through your grooming, including manicured nails, trimmed mustache and beard, lack of a five-o'clock shadow, neat and attractive hair and the right amount of makeup and jewelry that can be seen and not heard.

Creativity

While some jobs allow more creative expression than others, all of them permit you to individualize at least a bit. Express your uniqueness through a special tie and matching hankie, a scarf or a special or exquisite piece of jewelry.

Reliability

The sum of the above adds up to how reliable you are from the big picture to the details. Can you be counted on to look and behave in a professional manner wherever your job takes you?

Dress Codes

Dress codes are different by industry and by geography. While casual dress may be okay for inside jobs, if you get a job working face to face with customers, the rules are different. The Rule of Thumb is always to dress one level above what is customary for your industry. There is no penalty for overdressing, but there is always a penalty for dressing below your customer's attire.

East Coast, West Coast

East Coast clients are different from West Coast clients. Silicon Valley employees don't think twice about showing up in shorts and wearing sandals. That would not go over too well in Boston or Philadelphia. Salespeople with East Coast clients should only wear a tie when their clients wear one too, for example, when calling on a law firm, calling on Wall Street bankers, etc.

If you go into sales, remember that a big part of selling is showmanship. That means show up, dress up, and keep up a positive attitude.[2]

---

[2] *Look Good to Sell Well*, Gerhard Gschwandtner. Selling Power Magazine, January/February 2007

Tip 15

Grow Your Network.

Grow Your Network.

Without knowing it, you have been making contacts and building your personal network your entire life. Now that you are in corporate America, you should focus on growing your network. Why? Because networking gives you an advantage in knowing people who:

- Can hook you up with job opportunities
- Introduce you to influential people
- Serve as references for you
- Help you understand the politics of an organization
- Help you find mentors

How to Increase Your Network

Join your corporate affinity groups. In addition to a group that matches your comfort level (Black, Women, Latino, Asian, Gay/Lesbian, Native American, and Disabled); I suggest you join other affinity groups. You should understand their issues and attend their functions. Remember, too, that they know people who could help your career.

Use the Internet to increase both your networking skills and your personal network. Two of my favorites are Linked In and PLAXO. I have access to thousands of professional people. Check them out at www.linkedin.com and www.plaxo.com.

Join professional organizations that match your career discipline. There are organizations for women, engineers, writers, MBA's, architects, scientists, and on and on. Don't be afraid to join the leadership of these organizations. This gives you the opportunity to build your leadership and team-building skills.

Tip 16

Don't be a Clock Watcher.

Don't be a Clock Watcher.

Your paycheck is probably based on a 40-hour week. Unless you work at home, you are expected to take a 45-minute to one-hour lunch. Unlike college, where you could head out of the classroom when the bell rang, in corporate America you are expected to work as long as it takes to get a task done. If your hours are 8 a.m. to 5 p.m., the worst habit you can develop is to always head out the door at 5 p.m. every day.

Understand that you are always being watched. Your manager, your team and, in some cases, your customers measure your professionalism by your end-of-day attitude. Professionals do not watch the clock. If there is work to be done, you work until it is done.

Of course, there will be days when you have commitments. It is important to have a work-life balance. But the person who catches management's eye for promotion is the person who understands and accepts crunch time and works accordingly.

Here is a caveat. I knew some folks in corporate America who always worked until about 9 p.m. or 10 p.m. practically every day, but never showed effective results. They expected management to appreciate how much time they were spending in the office. Sure, they looked busy all the time, but without any measurable results, they had nothing to offer to improve their image with management. If anything, they proved to be a management annoyance because at performance review time, they expected to get points for spending so much time in the office. Some even wanted to be compensated with time off or extra pay. It does not work that way, folks. Excel at your commitments by measuring your time accordingly.

Tip 17

Congratulate the Success of Others Without Resentment.

Congratulate the Success of Others without Resentment.

Count on this...someone will get a promotion, accolades, or special mention at a department meeting. You may be thinking that the glory should be yours, not theirs. You feel you worked as hard as that person did. You are a team player and a leader. You sacrificed some personal time to help make a project successful. How come someone other than you is getting so much praise?

For every scenario, there are probably 10 or more possibilities as to why this is happening. The honoree may have offered creative solutions that increased departmental productivity. The honoree may be working closer with management than you. The honoree could be the president's niece or nephew. Or, this situation could just fall into the life-is-unfair bucket.

Regardless of the reason, you probably do not have all the facts. You should have only one response and that is to congratulate the honoree. Assuming you decide to resent the attention the honoree is getting and you let others know that you are upset about this, you can bet you are on the road to being listed on management's high maintenance list. This means management considers you to be a pain in the butt and is turned off by your complaining. Your unprofessional behavior gives off vibes that tell management that you are not a team player, are a self-centered whiner, negative, and not a candidate for a leadership position. I have known people who were next in line for a promotion, but were taken off the list because of their resentful behavior.

According to an article titled Fool's goal in The New & Observer "Career Builder" section (April 1, 2007), no one wants to work with an arrogant employee who steals ideas or an egotistical worker who demeans others. Helping your co-workers doesn't make you a pushover — it makes you smart. Likeable employees move up the company ranks more quickly, and your colleagues will be more likely to help you find leads when you launch your next job search.

Just say, "Congratulations!" with a smile and continue the positive discussions with management for your career.

Tip 18

Be a Risk Taker.

Be a Risk Taker.

Many people who have had the most success took non-traditional paths to the top. You can do the same by following opportunities, not being rigid when considering your next move and taking chances.

After you have spent at least a few years in your company and assuming you have access to upper management, ask yourself: Do you have a great idea about a role you could fill for your company? Research it, write a proposal and present it to your manager. The company might consider it. If nothing else, your managers will notice your willingness to take initiative and you've made a strong, positive statement. As a result, they might remember you the next time they're giving out bonuses or promoting people.

Tip 19

Set Realistic
Ambitions.

Set Realistic Ambitions.

Years ago I knew a gentleman whose goal was to become a corporate pilot. There was just one problem. He had never flown a plane. Yet, he was completely serious when he talked to management about his career ambitions.

I know of others who were fanatic about getting into management. That is a reasonable goal, but the people in question did not like working with people. They considered people to be annoying. The only reason they wanted to be managers was because they heard an employee has more opportunities after being a manager.

Your ambitions should be in line with your personality, your experience, your skills, and the potential your mentors see for you.

Unrealistic ambitions set you up for frustration and disappointment. Having a mentor can help keep you on track. Remember to be open to constructive criticism.

Tip 20

Keep Your
Manager Happy.

Keep your Manager Happy.

It is bound to happen. One day you will be stuck with an arrogant, sarcastic, mean-spirited manager. So what do you do? Like it or not, the better your manager feels, the better you'll be treated.

If you are willing to make the effort without selling your soul or being labeled a brown-noser, study your manager to make sure you have a good idea of what makes your manager happy. Is he or she a sports fan? What college did they attend? Do they like to cook? Do they have a special place in their hearts for their family? Once you find out, be sure to find an opportunity to start a conversation focusing on what makes your manager happy.

Do not be intimidated. The more professional you act the more respect your manager will have for you. When problems arise, talk them out with your manager.

Again referring the The News & Observer's "Career Builder" section, "Whether your pay is too low, the work is tedious or you think your boss is an idiot, be careful of who hears you complain. If it gets back to your boss, she may just put you out of your misery.

Tip 21

Beware Delusions
of Grandeur.

Beware Delusions of Grandeur.

A spin-off of having realistic ambitions is avoiding delusions of grandeur. I use that term to describe people who feel they are entitled to promotions to executive levels even though they haven't followed the advice listed in this book to succeed in corporate America. They cast aspersions on others who surpass them and resent seeing others get promoted.

I have seen married couples resent it when their spouse moves to a higher position, even though the spouse did everything correctly to earn the promotion. This is a sickness that destroys relationships. One hundred percent of the people I know who suffer from delusions of grandeur have been kicked out of their jobs in corporate America. Some move to other corporations, but it is always a matter of time before they are asked to leave the new company for the same reasons. If they had just spent as much energy doing the tips listed in this book instead of complaining about the success of others, they could have achieved the success they coveted.

My advice: Don't give lip service to the tips in this book. Learn and apply.

Tip 22

Manage Your Credit. Don't go Crazy When You get Your First Paycheck.

Manage your Credit. Don't Go Crazy when you get Your First Paycheck.

When you were in college, what was your typical meal? Many students tell me they eat Hot Pockets™, Lean Pockets™, Ramen Noodles™, and other quick and inexpensive meals. Money was tight and there was little time for a sit-down meal. Does this sound like your experience?

Now, you are in corporate America and you received your first paycheck. It's probably more money than you have had in your hands EVER. Your first impulse may be to spend, spend, and spend some more. You want to decorate your new apartment, stock the refrigerator, look for a new car, buy new clothes, treat some friends to dinner, get a big-screen television (probably HDTV), purchase the latest cell phone and some DVDs, buy a new laptop and scope the web for the latest electronic gizmos.

STOP. Instead of focusing on all these materialistic things, how about doing some long-term planning?

The first thing you should do before you even get your first paycheck is to enroll in your company's 401K plan. Find out the maximum allowable contribution and go for it. I promise you that if you start your corporate life by contributing to the 401K at the maximum contribution, you will be building an amazing nest egg. Your nest egg will eventually get you into your first home (and out of an apartment), which is a practical investment. Your company probably offers an on-line estimator to show you how fast your money can grow. If you can't afford to contribute the maximum allowed, find out what percentage your company matches and contribute that amount as a starting point.

The mistake I made was focusing on enjoying my new-found wealth with no regard to savings. By the time I joined my company's 401K, I was thousands of dollars behind where I could have been. Better late than never, though. I was careful to diversify my investments (avoid an Enron situation or investing 100% in the corporation you work for).

I don't want to scare you (well, maybe I **do** want to scare you) with the following advice. As you start your journey into corporate life, many of you are full of glee that your financial troubles are over. Once again, you should consider long-term goals. In 60 years as you enter your 80s, a loaf of bread may cost $25 or more. It's called inflation. If you haven't invested and saved wisely, you may find yourself having to share cat food with Fluffy in order to eat. You may have to decide between ordering your prescription medicines and paying your rent.

In the 1990s, people had high incomes and re-tirement plans for life. But corporations are no longer see-ing the huge profits and salaries. Bonuses are reduced. Couples who did well in the 1990's, before the Internet bubble burst, had gorgeous mini-mansions for themselves and their children complete with multiple cars and plenty of spending money.

But now the children are older and are still living at home because they are discovering that the entry-level jobs don't pay what their parents made. The children can-not afford to live on their own. They can't afford the flashy car, their own home, or the great meals they can enjoy with their parents. So, the parents continue to pay for the entire family at a time when they thought they'd be empty nesters with extra time and money.

Now, let's get back to you and your situation. As-suming you get married and raise a family, what will your financial situation be like in 20 years and beyond? If you squander your money in the early years of working in cor-porate America, do not invest in your company's 401K plan, do not have a Plan B if you get laid off, don't work with a financial advisor, and hope that Power Ball will be the answer to all your financial problems, you may find yourself working well into your 80s just to survive.

On a brighter note, you have an advantage. You are reading this book and, if you follow the advice, you have a head start to success. Follow my advice. Think long term and grow rich.

Section 2. Life is Unfair.

You follow all the tips and you expect to be promoted to higher levels within the corporation. Oops. Something happens and all your dreams go up in smoke. Now what do you do? Here are some tips to help you plan for that oops moment.

Tip 23

Nourish an Entrepreneurial Spirit.

Nourish an Entrepreneurial Spirit.

You had better sit down for these blatant statements. Ready? Corporations do not love you. Corporations exist to make money and please their shareholders. Employees are expendable; outsourcing is a proven method to reduce corporate expenses. There are CEOs who have MBAs and Ph.D.s but do not know how to keep their corporations profitable.

With this in mind, you might want to always have a Plan B in case your job gets cut. Your Plan B is your protection to ensure you can put food on your table and still pay your bills. Think about what business you'd own if you were on your own.

Do your homework to:
- Understand your market
- Create your business model
- Create your five-year marketing plan
- Understand what SBA (Small Business Administration) can do for you
- Find a CPA
- Work with a financial planner to create a financial plan for your business with sound investments
- Protect your credit rating
- Build up savings to carry you over for at least six months

My friend Byron B. is a large fellow who decided that there are a lot of big men who need hip-hop shirts. Byron formed a company to create hip-hop clothes for big and tall men. He is a star within corporate America who has the entrepreneurial spirit.

My friend Sharon L. and her husband love to cook. She has an MBA and an entrepreneurial spirit. While working in corporate America, she and her family opened Wings 'N Things – a partnership of friends specializing in wings and fries served for outdoor venues. After that they opened Motherland Foods making snack foods that are marketed to a black audience.

Be careful. Refer to Tip 21, *Beware Delusions of Grandeur.* I also have corporate friends who did not do their homework and decided to open companies because they wanted to have CEO behind their names. One hundred percent of them failed. Most of them didn't know how to balance their checkbooks. Do you know how to balance your checkbook? If not, get Quicken,™ which does the work for you. Go to a bank and ask a bank officer to teach you how to balance your checkbook. None of this will work unless you keep track of all the checks you write and items you buy with your debit card.

If you start your Plan B, while still either in college or while in corporate America, follow through with solid marketing research and financial planning, and do NOT let it interfere with your corporate job, then you will be successful.

Tip 24

Identify with Your Company, but Don't get Brainwashed.

Identify with your Company, but Don't Get Brainwashed.

I'm guilty of this. I was so proud of the corporation I worked for that when people asked me what I did, I responded by just saying the name of the corporation I worked for. The corporation had instilled this in all of us. We felt like a family. I expected to work for that one corporation forever, as did thousands of others.

Then, the climate changed and the corporation had to change or suffer extreme business losses. Many people in the corporation could not handle the change. It reminded me of a case years ago involving an NBA player who got to play for one season and then was released. He committed suicide. He identified himself so much as an NBA player, that without his job with the NBA, he thought he had no point in living. Some corporate stories are very similar. Corporate change has led to depression, divorce, alcoholism, drug use and poverty, all because the employees identified too closely with the corporation.

Think of yourself as an entrepreneur or consultant to protect yourself and maintain your sanity. Don't expect to work for one company forever. Of course, you have to provide loyalty and value to the company paying you. Loyalty is healthy and encouraged, but in the end, it won't help a lot. (Apathy is worse and could get you released from the company sooner.)

Follow the advice in this book to be successful in corporate America, but remember to always have your Plan B in case you need to find another source of employment.

Tip 25

Interview with
Other Companies
to Understand
Your Value.

Interview with Other Companies to Understand Your Value.

After two or three years with a company, you may wonder if you are earning an annual salary that is in line with the national average for those with your same skills. Are you having trouble understanding what skills companies covet from new graduates?

One way to find out is to interview with other companies. Your goal is not to get hired. Your goal is to understand if you are marketable. Be honest with your interviewer by letting him or her know you want a courtesy interview to understand your marketability. Ask for 30 minutes to one hour and stick to that timeframe. People are busy and appreciate it when your respect their time.

After the interview, review your notes to validate if you need to take classes or attend seminars to increase your skills.

You are not betraying your company if you set up interviews with other companies. Just don't broadcast that you are validating your marketability. If you do, your management team may decide to put you on the short-term list thinking that you will leave soon.

Tip 26

Keep Your Resumé
Current.

Keep Your Resumé Current.

Hopefully, you used your college career center to help you prepare your first resumé. After you enter corporate America, update your resume annually.

Add the following:

☐ Leadership positions
☐ Teamwork successes
☐ Accolades
☐ Technical advances
☐ Patents
☐ Publications
☐ Any important accomplishments that set you apart from others

Send updated resumés to the companies for your courtesy interviews.

Tip 27

Be Ready to Handle Challenges.

Be Ready to Handle Challenges.

Just as the sun rises in the east, you can expect to have days at work that are unbearable because of politics, bad management, friction between you and co-workers, or a full moon. My grandmother always told me, "You get more flies with honey than you do with vinegar." That means you have to train yourself on how to handle rough situations so that you come out a winner and maintain the respect people have for you.

Start by documenting situations that you suspect might go awry and lead to conflict. Use dates and names. Write what occurred that seemed odd or unprofessional. Your goal is to protect yourself in case all fingers point to you as having made a terrible mistake.

Face-to-face conversations are always valuable, but in case you need to send an e-mail about a situation, remember the following tips:

- ❑ Avoid personally attacking someone directly. It is very costly. Omit your feelings. Just list the facts. Focus on the issue, not the person.

- ❑ State your commitment. For example, let's say that you are a team leader and a team member botched testing for a new program because he didn't follow the company protocol as you'd instructed. Now, you're wrongly being blamed for the problem. Start your e-mail by stating: "I am committed to our company's quality goals and testing protocol." List your facts. End with your commitment by saying how you will rectify the situation and assure it will not recur.

- ❑ State your concerns and how they relate to your commitment. Let's say, for the sake of this example, you had mentioned to your manager that the team member consistently ignores company protocol, even though you have been urging him to do so. If you have kept records, this is the time in your e-mail to list the dates you talked to both the team member and management about this problem.

❑ State a clear request that is needed and by when. If your solution is to have team training to review the company's testing protocol, ask that management approve half-day training by a certain date.

❑ State what your actions will be if you do not get a response to your e-mail. This must be non-threatening. If management doesn't respond to approve the half-day team training by the date you requested, send a reminder note. You have a choice. You can say, "I assume no response is an agreement to my request." Or, you can walk into your manager's office to discuss how to finalize the situation. Regardless of what you do, protect yourself. Don't fly off the handle. Control your emotions. Win people over with positive statements, facts, and professionalism. (You can always go home and punch a hole in the wall when you are alone.)

Section 3. Diversity in Corporate America.

The following article appeared in *Essence*, January 2007 issue.

"A new study shows that diversity training used by U.S. corporations has failed to increase the number of minorities in management. We're shocked — who would have thought that Kumbaya icebreaker activities and *Let's Talk Diversity!* videos wouldn't be enough?"

Keep that in mind as you read these tips.

This section targets minority students who may have issues with succeeding in corporate America.

Tip 28

Rethink Old-School Advice.

126

Rethink Old-School Advice.

"Education opens all doors, honey. Just get your diploma and you'll be set for life."

"Once you get into corporate America, just keep your head down, do your job, and don't make waves."

"Pride goeth before the fall, baby. Stay humble and don't brag on yourself."

Anyone who gives you any of the advice listed above is full of good intentions and wants only the best for you. But after 20+ years in corporate America, I declare to you today that such advice is wrong. Having the education to qualify for a job does not guarantee long-term success.

You must get out of your comfort zone of expecting success just by doing a good job. In addition to producing outstanding results, not being afraid to work overtime, and showing leadership, you must work closely with your management teams just as your white counterparts do.

When you have produced outstanding results, let your management team know. For example, if customers send you a note congratulating you on getting their new system configured and operational in record time, forward that note to your management team. If a team member gives you high praise for helping him or her resolve an important business problem, ask them to send a note to your manager and copy you. Keep all notes of praise in a personal folder. You may need to refer to them at your performance reviews.

Tip 29

Play the Game,
but Don't Sell Out.

Play the Game, but Don't Sell Out.

I define selling out as violating your principles and doing something uncomfortable for monetary or social gain. During my research, some of my research participants expressed a discomfort in doing what it takes to get ahead in corporate America, stating they didn't want to sell out.

Here is an excerpt from what one participant said: "The single greatest challenge was having to set aside some of my cultural norms and sometimes my value system. Corporate culture requires some degree of self-centeredness, insincerity, and boastfulness that goes against the core of my value system. Corporate culture also requires friendships of convenience. People I had eaten lunch with every day no longer speak to me now that I have no influence on their career because we no longer work on the same projects anymore. These networks are required for success but they are often not real friendships. For young African-Americans entering corporate America, this could be quite confusing. Normally, in the black culture when we befriend somebody, it is not for a purpose. It is because we have something in common and we like each other."

"In the corporate culture it is very different. That was something I really had to get adjusted to. When a problem comes up that I don't know how to deal with, I can find the person who has the skill that I need. I don't call it friendship. I call it relationships of convenience."

The participant used his skill to tolerate people that he considered hypocritical to use them to his advantage. He maintained an extended network because he knew that when he became a manager, he'd need to call upon them for their expertise. He has since become a successful and respected manager by not selling out. He had lines that people knew not to cross. He kept his private life to himself, but didn't hesitate to ask others about their lives because he knew people loved to talk about themselves.

His behavior made him appear friendly and non-threatening.

Tip 30

Involve Yourself with Your Team (from the Diverse Perspective).

Involve Yourself with Your Team (from the Diverse Perspective).

Yes, I did discuss this earlier in the book. Let me take the discussion a bit further.

One of my research participants said, "A lot of minority new hires come in from different cities and have lost their circle of friends and support. They are dumped into a place by themselves. How they fit in, and who they choose to be with, is touchy. They have a harder time fitting in and even though we don't want to admit it, there are still stereotypes about minorities."

The challenge is figuring out how to involve yourself with your team. Here are tips that were given to me by one of my mentors:

❑ If the team goes out for drinks, go with them. You don't have to drink alcohol. Order club soda with lemon or order regular sodas.

❑ Only stay for 90 minutes. This shows you are a team player because you showed up. This especially applies to women. After 90 minutes drinkers can get rowdy. You don't want to be there.

❑ Let the others do most of the talking. Yes, you'd be amazed at personal information people are open to sharing.

❑ Mingle. Talk to a person or group for five to seven minutes and move on to the next person or group.

❑ When going to a sports bar, have fun, especially if you are into the game. Just control how much you drink.

Tip 31

Be Aware of Your Three Languages.

Be Aware of Your Three Languages.

Are you aware that you have different languages based upon your audience?

1. When you are with your friends, you probably use slang and popular terms. It's fun and cool.

2. Do you use the same language with your family? Probably not. If you have respect for your parents, grandparents, aunts and uncles, you speak to them in the language they use. This is the language you use when you are in church.

3. In corporate America you should use the language of business especially when you are giving a presentation, talking to decision-makers and your mentors. Here is where the comfort level of others is important. You should communicate on a level that keeps everyone comfortable. How do you do this? Listen to how other professionals speak. Listen to those you admire and consider successful in the corporation and take your cues from them.

Tip 32

Don't Laugh
at Off-Color
or Racist Jokes.

Don't Laugh at Off-Color or Racist Jokes.

You must maintain your dignity at all times. If those around you start telling off-color, sexist, bawdy, or racist jokes, do not laugh. If you do, you are selling out. The best book to read on this subject is, *"Ouch! That Stereotype Hurts"* by Leslie Aguilar. The book provides invaluable tips for handling delicate situations.

Tip 33

Use INROADS to get Your Internship.

Use INROADS to get your Internship.

If your school's career center works with IN-ROADS, please, please check it out.

The mission of INROADS is to develop and place talented minority youth in business and industry and prepare them for corporate and community leadership.

INROADS seeks high-performing Black, Hispanic/Latino, and Native American Indian students for internship opportunities with some of the nation's largest companies. Its rigorous career development training process will challenge you to commit to excellence and raise the bar on your personal expectations.

Section 4. Quirky Tips for Consideration.

Tip 34

Get Your Sleep.

Get Your Sleep.

To be your best, you've got to work hard, but you should also get your sleep. Sleep is a type of unconsciousness and is a state of being unaware of the world. Sleep is essential to good health as it refreshes the body and the mind. If you get enough sleep regularly every night you will feel and be able to work better.

How much sleep should a person get each night? The answer depends on the individual. Some people need a great deal of sleep, while others require only a minimum of sleep. The individual needs to get the amount of sleep necessary to feel alert, healthy, and totally fit. If you are dragging during the day, you need to get more sleep. Nervous and tense people usually require more sleep than those of a placid disposition. The average individual maintains his health with about eight hours of sleep.

The hazards of sleep deprivation are many, increased irritability, loss of appetite, lethargy, slowing of reflexes and depression to name a few.

Tip 35

Learn to Play Golf.

Learn to Play Golf.

Golf, the unchallenged heart of the old-boy business network, isn't just for men anymore. Now, women are beginning to reap the same benefits found on the green. Lots of networking is done on the golf course. People will have a chance to get to know you in a comfortable and relaxed setting.

When your company holds a golf outing, you can join right in. Don't be too aggressive in selling yourself. Let those with the power lead the discussions. Be up to date on current affairs, avoid talking about national or local politics, and most importantly, understand what is happening with your corporation, the marketplace, and your company's competitors. Doing so will prepare you for any discussions.

Be sure you don't come off as a brown-noser. Just be your professional self and leave a good impression with others.

Section 5. Final Thoughts.

Some of you may consider corporations to be evil. You may think they are full of greedy executives who are not interested in helping the world.

In fairness, if you read *Fortune* Magazine and other business journals, you'll find that many corporations are charitable and caring. For example, corporations like IBM and Cisco participate heavily in charities. They sent people to the Gulf Coast after Hurricane Katrina to set up online access so people could e-mail their families to say they were okay. Cisco sent equipment to schools in Middle-Eastern countries suffering from the aftermath of wars and terrorists. Many corporations have employees who participate in local charities, like Habitat for Humanity.

Sure, there are horror stories about corruption and deceit with corporations like Enron, WorldCom, and others, but there are even more positive stories about companies like Starbucks that provides benefits for 100% of its employees, even if they are part-time.

Research your corporation of choice to ensure it meets with your ethical standards. Make sure you are clear on what you see as your life mission. This is a process and not a one-time exercise. It is about coming up with a mission for your life. If you invest time in living that mission, it will be a lantern and a shield for you. I am living my mission by sharing the information I learned to help others.

Good luck to you.